LYSISTRATA

Other English versions
by Dudley Fitts and Robert Fitzgerald

THE ALCESTIS OF EURIPIDES

THE ANTIGONE OF SOPHOCLES

THE OEDIPUS REX OF SOPHOCLES

ARISTOPHANES

LYSISTRATA

AN ENGLISH VERSION
BY DUDLEY FITTS

HARCOURT, BRACE AND COMPANY
NEW YORK

Library of Congress Catalog Card Number: 54-6389

for FREDERICK *and* LEE PETERSON

ποῖ λευκὸν ἵππον

INTRODUCTORY NOTE

I

Aristophanes wrote *Lysistrata* in 412 B.C. and produced it early in the following year at the Lenaia, the great Athenian festival of Dionysos. It is the last of the three comedies which the poet devoted to the subject of the Peloponnesian War; and, in spite of its almost unexampled ribaldry, it has a sombre depth, an intensity of meaning, that we do not find in the other two plays, the *Acharnians* and the *Peace*. And rightly; for the *Lysistrata* was composed less than a year after Athens had learned of the failure of the great Sicilian Expedition—a military disaster which (as even Aristophanes could not see) meant the end of Athenian civilization. True, the final collapse at Aigospotomoi was seven years in the future; but that battle was merely Waterloo, whereas the man-draining Sicilian fiasco was that of Napoleon's Grand Army at Moscow in 1812. *Lysistrata,* then, was written in a time of despair. It is notable among war plays for the courage with which the poet faces that despair and braves the popular hatred which any man must endure when he utters an unpopular truth in a black hour. The bravery disguises itself as fun, a wry solution, a way out—the women of the warring nations are to go on a marital strike until peace has been restored. This is an interesting idea, and it gives us a great deal of indecorous horseplay in the complications of the plot; an idea too simple for Aristophanes' time or for our own; an idea, nevertheless, which has its possibilities.

If a statesman today were to suggest seriously, not merely as a rhetorical sop to liberalism, that human survival depends upon international concession, each country yielding its sacred Sovereignty to the common good, I suspect that he would be hooted into silence. Let us imagine that such a dreamer (we always call them dreamers) were to propose what Aristophanes proposes in this play: That for the sake of world peace we should cede Long Island to Venezuela, dependent, of course, upon an equal (if possible) cession by Venezuela; and that we should, moveover, abolish the huge armies on both sides, institute an international police force, and devote the rest of our lives to a real inter-American amity. One's brain staggers at the thought; but I fancy that the only way for such a dreamer to escape lynching would be to present his idea disguised as a dream, or as a marvelous farce.

And this is what Aristophanes did. The *Lysistrata* is both farce and dream. It is generally held to be indecent, but too much has been made of the indecency. What is indecency? It is indecent in some respectable parts of the world to eat food in company. Elsewhere it is indecent to wear shoes when you go to church. Sexual indecency is a particularly touchy subject among us, who are the heirs of a long tradition of sexual indecency. The word itself finally blurs. But this much is true: the indecency of which we complain in Aristophanes (and in Rabelais, and in Chaucer, and in Shakspere) is not a leering indecency; it has nothing to do with our cultivated concept of Sin. Partly for ritualistic reasons (since the Dionysos myth is a fertility myth), the phallic element is everywhere in the comedies of Aristophanes. But something else is at work. The phallic joke may be ritualistic; but it is also funny, and healthily funny. To us, a dirty joke is a dirty joke, something to be sniggered at; to Aristophanes, it was something indecorous—since the situation involves men and women at their least decorous moments—, but it was something to be guffawed at in the open air of the Theatre. And since this innocent rough laughter is the great dissolvent, the great anodyne, he wisely chose it to mitigate his seriousness. I do not see what else he could have done.

II

When Robert Fitzgerald and I made our version of the *Antigonê*, we used as epigraph this observation by Roger Bacon:

Et quod propriè dicitur in idiomate Picardorum horrescit apud Burgundos, immò apud Gallicos viciniores; quantò igitur magis accidet hoc apud linguas diversas! Quapropter quod bene factum est in una lingua non est possibile ut transferatur in aliam secundum ejus proprietatem quam habuerit in priori.

I repeat the quotation now, not because I admire its Latinity—indeed, it is very queasy Latin—, but because it embodies a truth with which every translator of poetry must live: *It can't be done.* A disheartening challenge; yet a man must rise to it, and I shall try to describe my own attempts to circumvent Friar Bacon.

Early in our work upon our first translation, the *Alkestis* of

Euripides, Fitzgerald and I discovered that it was useless to attempt an approximation of the original metres. I am aware that many translators have tried to do so; but to my ear their result is only that unnatural stiffness which is the death of poetry. And nothing is more dead than dead poetry, however it may be tricked out on the printed page. We chose then what I have chosen for my *Lysistrata*, in the non-choral passages: a very free five-stress line, highly counterpointed, admitting all kinds of variation and distortion. The result was ambiguous: one eminent critic complained that he could detect no metre at all, while another, equally eminent, held that we had contributed a new metre to American verse. However that may be, our intention was, first and foremost, to be *sayable;* for poetry is not a matter of reading, but of hearing. The choruses, however, presented a different problem; we attacked them in all sorts of ways, and I do not know with what success. At any rate, I have carried over our method in translating the choruses of *Lysistrata*. Aristophanes is one of the most fluent and expressive of lyrists; but in this play, barring the songs at the end, there is almost nothing of the lyric *élan* that characterizes his *Birds* and his *Clouds*. Consequently, I have felt free to experiment, using metre, rime, assonance, phonic inversion—all the tricks, in short, at my limited disposal; and this, I must warn the reader, does not result in strict translation.

Nevertheless, faithful translation has been my aim. In general, this version is as closely *ad litteram expressa* as I could make it. There are inevitable exceptions: let one represent the others. Thus, at line 158, Kalonikê urgently asks

x

What if [our men] just get up and leave us?

Lysistrata answers her with a brutal phrase from one Pherekratês, a comic poet whose works are unhappily lost to us. 'We'll have to skin a skinned dog' is the general sense; but what does that mean to us? The commentators helpfully inform us that this is the equivalent of Plautus's *nudo detrahere vestimenta,* and the formidable Brunck is even more explicit: Lysistrata, he says, *penem coriaceum intelligit.* It seems obvious that Pherekratês's little obscenity cannot stand by itself in translation. It demands either a footnote or a paraphrase. My rendering, therefore, while not 'faithful,' is an attempt at a comparable indelicacy in terms of our own speech.

I have used the Oxford text established by Hall and Geldart, and the line numbers at the top of the pages accord with that. Yet I have not been slavish: when I felt the need to depart from authority, I departed. Thus, in the *éxodos,* I have introduced an Athenian Drunkard. He wandered in one afternoon, and I liked him and kept him; but you will not find him in any of the texts. Or, rather, you will find him in various guises: as a duo, Athenian I and Athenian II; or as something vaguely given to the Chorus; or as what-not. It seemed to me legitimate, given the uncertainty of the text, to create a character of whom I think Aristophanes would have approved. And there are other passages where a redistribution of the conventional parts forced itself upon my imagination. Less defensible, I suppose, is my use of a deep-South accent for the speakers from Lakonia. In this, however, I am tamely following tradition. The translations with which I am acquainted render these speeches either in thick *Scots* or in a kind of never-never Devonshire. The distinction between Attic and Doric must obviously be made. It is my hope, in the unlikely event that this play ever reaches the stage, that my Spartan men and women will not speak these lines trippingly on the tongue, but in the kind of blackface minstrel dialect which only Mr E. E. Cummings and the better burlesk houses have preserved in our day.

III

Ecce quàm bonum et salutare, says the Psalmist, *fratres habitare in unum!* I take this to be the meaning of *Lysistrata*; at any rate, it has worked out so in the process of composition. The translation, begun in summer idleness, rapidly became a community project, and my indebtedness is vast. I shall not attempt here to thank all of my collaborators. Nevertheless, I must signalize my wife; Mr and Mrs Frederick Peterson, *animæ naturaliter Aristophanicæ*; Mr and Mrs Alan Blackmer; Robert Fitzgerald, from whom I have learned whatever I know about the translation of poetry; Mr and Mrs Francis McCarthy; and Miss Meredith Thiras, for her devoted help in preparing the manuscript for publication.

DF

CONTENTS

PERSONS REPRESENTED:

LYSISTRATA	MAGISTRATE
KALONIKE	KINESIAS
MYRRHINE	SPARTAN HERALD
LAMPITO	SPARTAN AMBASSADOR
CHORUS	A SENTRY

ATHENIAN DRUNKARD

SCENE: Athens. First, a public square; later, beneath the walls of the Akropolis; later, a courtyard within the Akropolis. Time: early in 411 B.C.

Until the *éxodos,* the CHORUS is divided into two hemichori: the first, of Old Men; the second, of Old Women. Each of these has its CHORAGOS. In the *éxodos,* the hemichori return as Athenians and Spartans

The supernumeraries include the BABY SON of Kinesias; STRATYLLIS, a member of the hemichorus of Old Women; various individual speakers, both Spartan and Athenian.

PROLOGUE

[*Athens; a public square; early morning;* LYSISTRATA
sola

LYSISTRATA:

If someone had invited them to a festival—
Bacchos's, say, or Pan's, or Aphroditê's, or
that Genetyllis business—, you couldn't get through the streets,
what with the drums and the dancing. But now,
not a woman in sight!

                Except—oh, yes!

                       [*Enter* KALONIKE

Here's one, at last. Good
morning, Kalonikê.

KALONIKE:

              Good morning, Lysistrata.

                           Darling,
don't frown so! You'll ruin your face!

LYSISTRATA:

                       Never mind my face.

Kalonikê,
the way we women behave! Really, I don't blame the men
for what they say about us.

KALONIKE:

              No; I imagine they're right.

LYSISTRATA:

For example: I call a meeting

3

to think out a most important matter—and what happens?
The women all stay in bed!

KALONIKE:

                                   Oh, they'll be along.
It's hard to get away, you know: a husband, a cook,
a child . . . Home life can be *so* demanding!

LYSISTRATA:

What I have in mind is even more demanding.

KALONIKE:

Tell me: what is it?

LYSISTRATA:

                          Something big.

KALONIKE:

                                   Goodness! *How* big?

LYSISTRATA:

Big enough for all of us.

KALONIKE:

                          But we're not all here!

LYSISTRATA:

We would be, if *that's* what was up!

                                   No, Kalonikê,
this is something I've been turning over for nights;
and, I may say, sleepless nights.

KALONIKE:

                          Can't be so hard, then,
if you've spent so much time on it.

4

LYSISTRATA:

Hard or not,
it comes to this: Only we women can save Greece!

KALONIKE:

Only we women? Poor Greece!

LYSISTRATA:

Just the same,
it's up to us. First, we must liquidate
the Peloponnesians—

KALONIKE:

Fun, fun!

LYSISTRATA:

—and then the Boiotians.

KALONIKE:

Oh! But not those heavenly eels!

LYSISTRATA:

You needn't worry.
Athens shall have her sea food. —But here's the point:
If we can get the women from those places
to join us women here, why, we can save
all Greece!

KALONIKE:

But dearest Lysistrata!
How can women do a thing so austere, so
political? We belong at home. Our only armor's
our transparent saffron dresses and
our pretty little shoes!

5

LYSISTRATA:

That's it exactly.
Those transparent saffron dresses, those little shoes—
well, there we are!

KALONIKE:

Oh?

LYSISTRATA:

Not a single man would lift
his spear—

KALONIKE:

I'll get my dress from the dyer's tomorrow!

LYSISTRATA:

—or need a shield—

KALONIKE:

The sweetest little negligée—

LYSISTRATA:

—or bring out his sword.

KALONIKE:

I know where I can buy
the dreamiest sandals!

LYSISTRATA:

Well, so you see. Now, shouldn't
the women have come?

KALONIKE:

Come? They should have *flown*!

LYSISTRATA:

Athenians are always late.

6

But imagine!

There's no one here from the South Shore.

KALONIKE:

They go to work early,

I can swear to that.

LYSISTRATA:

And nobody from Acharnai.

They should have been here hours ago!

KALONIKE:

Well, you'll get

that awful Theagenês woman: she's been having
her fortune told at Hekatê's shrine.

But look!

Someone at last! Can you see who they are?

[Enter MYRRHINE and other women

LYSISTRATA:

People from the suburbs.

KALONIKE:

Yes! The entire

membership of the Suburban League!

MYRRHINE:

Sorry to be late, Lysistrata.

Oh come,

don't scowl so! Say something!

LYSISTRATA:

My dear Myrrhinê,

7

what is there to say? After all,

you've been pretty casual about the whole thing.

MYRRHINE:

                                            Couldn't find

my girdle in the dark, that's all.

                              But what *is*

'the whole thing'?

LYSISTRATA:

Wait for the rest of them.

KALONIKE:

                          I suppose so. But, look!

Here's Lampitô!

                    [*Enter* LAMPITO *with women from Sparta*

LYSISTRATA:

                    Darling Lampitô,

how pretty you are today! What a nice color!

Goodness, you look as though you could strangle a bull!

LAMPITO:

Ah think Ah could! It's the work-out

in the gym every day; and, of co'se that dance of ahs

where y' kick yo' own tail.

LYSISTRATA:

                    What lovely breasts!

LAMPITO:

Lawdy, when y' touch me lahk that,

Ah feel lahk a heifer at the altar!

LYSISTRATA:

And this young lady?

Where is she from?

LAMPITO:

Boiotia. Social-Register type.

LYSISTRATA:

Good morning, Boiotian. You're as pretty as green grass.

KALONIKE:

And if you look,
you'll find that the lawn has just been cut.

LYSISTRATA:

And this lady?

LAMPITO:

From Korinth. But a good woman.

LYSISTRATA:

Well, in Korinth

anything's possible.

LAMPITO:

But let's get to work. Which one of you
called this meeting, and why?

LYSISTRATA:

I did.

LAMPITO:

Well, then:

what's up?

MYRRHINE:

Yes, what *is* 'the whole thing,' after all?

9

LYSISTRATA:

I'll tell you. —But first, one question.

MYRRHINE:

Ask away!

LYSISTRATA:

It's your husbands. Fathers of your children. Doesn't it bother you
that they're always off with the Army? I'll stake my life,
not one of you has a man in the house this minute!

KALONIKE:

Mine's been in Thrace the last five months, keeping an eye
on that General.

MYRRHINE:

Mine's been in Pylos for seven.

LAMPITO:

And mahn,
whenever he gets a *dis*charge, he goes raht back
with that li'l ole speah of his, and enlists again!

LYSISTRATA:

And not the ghost of a lover to be found!
From the very day the war began—

those Milesians!

I could skin them alive!

—I've not seen so much, even,
as one of those devices they call Widow's Delight.
But there! What's important is: If I've found a way
to end the war, are you with me?

10

MYRRHINE:

I should *say* so!

Even if I have to pawn my best dress and
drink up the proceeds.

KALONIKE:

Me, too! Even if they split me
right up the middle, like a flounder.

LAMPITO:

Ah'm shorely with you.

Ah'd crawl up Taÿgetos on mah knees
if that'd bring peace.

LYSISTRATA:

Then here it is.
Women! Sisters!
If we really want our men to make an armistice,
we must be ready to give up—

MYRRHINE:

Give up what?

Quick, tell us!

LYSISTRATA:

But *will* you?

MYRRHINE:

We will, even if it kills us.

LYSISTRATA:

Then we must give up sleeping with our men.

[*Long silence*

11

Oh? So now you're sorry? Won't look at me?
Doubtful? Pale? All teary-eyed?

                          But come: be frank with me,
as I've certainly been with you. Will you do it?

MYRRHINE:

                                   I couldn't. No.

Let the war go on.

KALONIKE:

                Nor I. Let the war go on.

LYSISTRATA:

You, you little flounder,
ready to be split up the middle?

KALONIKE:

                        Lysistrata, no!
I'd walk through fire for you—you *know* I would!—, but don't
ask us to give up *that*! Why, there's nothing like it!

LYSISTRATA:

And you?

BOIOTIAN:

               No. I must say *I'd* rather walk through fire.

LYSISTRATA:

You little salamanders!
No wonder poets write tragedies about women.
All we want's a quick tumble!

                    But you from Sparta:
if you stand by me, we may win yet! Will you?
It means so much!

LAMPITO:

Ah sweah, it means *too* much!
By the Two Goddesses, it does! Asking a girl
to sleep—Heaven knows how long!—in a great big bed
with nobody there but herself! But Ah'll stay with you!
Peace comes first!

LYSISTRATA:

Spoken like a true Spartan!

KALONIKE:

But if—

oh dear!

—if we give up what you tell us to,
will there *be* any peace?

LYSISTRATA:

Why, mercy, of course there will!
We'll just sit snug in our very thinnest gowns,
perfumed and powdered from top to bottom, and those men
simply won't stand still! And when we say No,
they'll go out of their minds! And there's your peace.
You can take my word for it.

LAMPITO:

Ah seem to remember
that Colonel Menelaos threw his sword away
when he saw Helen's breast all bare.

KALONIKE:

But, goodness me!
What if they just get up and leave us?

LYSISTRATA:

Well,
we'd have to fall back on ourselves, of course.
But they won't.

KALONIKE:

What if they drag us into the bedroom?

LYSISTRATA:

Hang on to the door.

KALONIKE:

What if they slap us?

LYSISTRATA:

If they do, you'd better give in.
But be sulky about it. Do I have to teach you how?
You know there's no fun for men when they have to force you.
There are millions of ways of getting them to see reason.
Don't you worry: a man
doesn't like it unless the girl co-operates.

KALONIKE:

I suppose so. Oh, all right! We'll go along!

LAMPITO:

Ah imagine us Spahtans can arrange a peace. But you
Athenians! Why, you're just war-mongerers!

LYSISTRATA:

Leave that to me.
I know how to make them listen.

LAMPITO:

Ah don't see how.

14

After all, they've got their boats; and there's lots of money
piled up in the Akropolis.

LYSISTRATA:

The Akropolis? Darling,
we're taking over the Akropolis today!
That's the older women's job. All the rest of us
are going to the Citadel to sacrifice—you understand me?
And once there, we're in for good!

LAMPITO:

Whee! Up the rebels!

Ah can see you're a good strat*ee*gist.

LYSISTRATA:

Well, then, Lampitô,
let's take the oath.

LAMPITO:

Say it. We'll sweah.

LYSISTRATA:

This is it.
—But Lord! Where's our Inner Guard? Never mind.

—You see this
shield? Put it down there. Now bring me the victim's entrails.

KALONIKE:

But the oath?

LYSISTRATA:

You remember how in Aischylos' *Seven*
they killed a sheep and swore on a shield? Well, then?

KALONIKE:

But I don't see how you can swear for peace on a shield.

LYSISTRATA:

What else do you suggest?

KALONIKE:

Why not a white horse?
We could swear by that.

LYSISTRATA:

And where will you get a white horse?

KALONIKE:

I never thought of that. *What* can we do?

MYRRHINE:

I have it!
Let's set this big black wine-bowl on the ground
and pour in a gallon or so of Thasian, and swear
not to add one drop of water.

LAMPITO:

Ah lahk *that* oath!

LYSISTRATA:

Bring the bowl and the wine-jug.

KALONIKE:

Oh, what a simply *huge* one!

LYSISTRATA:

Set it down; and, women, place your hands on the gift-offering.

O Goddess of Persuasion! And thou, O Loving-cup!
Look upon this our sacrifice, and
be gracious!

16

KALONIKE:

It spills out like blood. How red and pretty it is!

LAMPITO:

And Ah must say it smells good.

MYRRHINE:

Let me swear first!

KALONIKE:

No, by Aphroditê, let's toss for it!

LYSISTRATA:

Lampitô: all of you women: come, touch the bowl,
and repeat after me:
I WILL HAVE NOTHING TO DO WITH MY HUS-
BAND OR MY LOVER

KALONIKE:

I will have nothing to do with my husband or my lover

LYSISTRATA:

THOUGH HE COME TO ME IN PITIABLE CONDI-
TION

KALONIKE:

Though he come to me in pitiable condition
(Oh Lysistrata! This is killing me!)

LYSISTRATA:

I WILL STAY IN MY HOUSE UNTOUCHABLE

KALONIKE:

I will stay in my house untouchable

LYSISTRATA:

IN MY THINNEST SAFFRON SILK

17

KALONIKE:

In my thinnest saffron silk

LYSISTRATA:

AND MAKE HIM LONG FOR ME.

KALONIKE:

And make him long for me.

LYSISTRATA:

I WILL NOT GIVE MYSELF

KALONIKE:

I will not give myself

LYSISTRATA:

AND IF HE CONSTRAINS ME

KALONIKE:

And if he constrains me

LYSISTRATA:

I WILL BE AS COLD AS ICE AND NEVER MOVE

KALONIKE:

I will be as cold as ice and never move

LYSISTRATA:

I WILL NOT LIFT MY SLIPPERS TOWARD THE CEILING

KALONIKE:

I will not lift my slippers toward the ceiling

LYSISTRATA:

OR CROUCH ON ALL FOURS LIKE THE LIONESS IN THE CARVING

KALONIKE:

Or crouch on all fours like the lioness in the carving

LYSISTRATA:

AND IF I KEEP THIS OATH LET ME DRINK FROM
THIS BOWL

KALONIKE:

And if I keep this oath let me drink from this bowl

LYSISTRATA:

IF NOT, LET MY OWN BOWL BE FILLED WITH
WATER.

KALONIKE:

If not, let my own bowl be filled with water.

LYSISTRATA:

You have all sworn?

MYRRHINE:

We have.

LYSISTRATA:

Then thus

I sacrifice the victim.

[Drinks largely

KALONIKE:

Save some for us!

Here's to you, darling, and to you, and to you! It's all
for us women.

[Loud cries off-stage

LAMPITO:

What's all *that* whoozy-goozy?

LYSISTRATA:

Just what I told you.
The older women have taken the Akropolis. Now you, Lampitô,
rush back to Sparta. We'll take care of things here. And
be sure you get organized!

The rest of you girls,
up to the Citadel: and mind you push in the bolts.

KALONIKE:

But the men? Won't they be after us?

LYSISTRATA:

Just you leave
the men to me. There's not fire enough in the world
to make me open *my* door.

KALONIKE:

I hope so, by Aphroditê!
At any rate,
let's remember the League's reputation for hanging on!

[*Exeunt*

PÁRODOS: CHORAL EPISODE

[*The hillside just under the Akropolis. Enter* CHORUS
OF OLD MEN *with burning torches and braziers;
much puffing and coughing*

CHORAGOS ^m:

Easy, Drakês, old friend! Don't skin your shoulders
with those damnable big olive-branches. What a job!

CHORUS ^m:

Forward, forward, comrades! Whew!   [STROPHE I
The things that old age does to you!
Neighbor Strymodoros, would you have thought it?
   We've caught it—
               And from women, too!
Women that used to board with us, bed with us—
Now, by the gods, they've got ahead of us,
Taken the Akropolis (Heaven knows why!),
Profanèd the sacred statuar-y,
          And barred the doors,
           The aggravating whores!

CHORAGOS ^m:

Come, Philourgos, quick, pile your brushwood
next to the wall there.
         These traitors to Athens and to us,
we'll fry each last one of them! And the very first
will be old Lykôn's wife.

CHORUS ^m:

By Deméter I swear it—(ouch!),   [ANTISTROPHE I
I'll not perform the Kleomenês-crouch!
How he looked—and a good soldier, too—
    When out he flew,
                          that filthy pouch
Of a body of his all stinking and shaggy,
Bare as an eel, except for the bag he
Covered his rear with. Lord, what a mess!
Never a bath in six years, I'd guess!
                  Unhappy Sparta,
                  With such a martyr!

CHORAGOS ^m:

What a siege, friends! Seventeen ranks strong
we stood at the Gate, and never a chance for a nap.
And all because of women, whom the gods hate
(and so does Euripidês).
                          It's enough to make a veteran
turn in his medals from Marathon!

CHORUS ^m:

Forward, men! Just up the hillside,   [STROPHE 2
    And we're there!
Keep to the path! A yoke of oxen
    Wouldn't care
        To haul this lumber. Mind the fire,

24

Or it'll die before we're higher!
Puff! Puff!
This smoke will strangle me, sure enough!

Holy Heraklês, I'm blinded,   [ANTISTROPHE 2
Sure as fate!
It's Lemnos-fire we've been toting;
And isn't it great
To be singed by this infernal flame?
(Lachês, remember the Goddess: for shame!)
Woof! Woof!
A few steps more, and we're under the roof!

CHORAGOS ᵐ:
It catches! It's blazing!
Down with your loads!
We'll sizzle 'em now,
By all the gods!
Vine-branches here, quick!
Light 'em up,
And in through the gate with 'em!
If that doesn't stop
Their nonsense—well,
We'll smoke 'em to Hell.
Ker*shoo*!
(What we really need
Is a grad-u-ate,

25

Top of his class,
From Samos Military State.
Achoo!)
Come, do
Your duty, you!
Pour out your braziers,
Embers ablaze!
But first, Gentlemen, allow me to raise
The paian:

> *Lady*
Victory, now
Assist thine adherents
Here below!
Down with women!
Up with men!
Iô triumphe!

CHORUS ^m:

Amen!

> [*Enter* CHORUS OF OLD WOMEN *on the walls of the
> Akropolis, carrying jars of water to extinguish the
> fire set by the* CHORUS OF OLD MEN

CHORAGOS ^w:

Fire, fire!
Quickly, quickly, women, if we're to save ourselves!

26

CHORUS ^w:

[STROPHE

> Nikodikê, run!
> Or Kalykê's done
> To a turn, and poor Kratylla's
> Smoked like a ham.
>
> Damn
>
> These men and their wars,
> Their hateful ways!
> I nearly died before I got to the place
> Where we fill our jars:
>> Slaves pushing and jostling—
>> Such a hustling
> I never saw in all my days!

[ANTISTROPHE

> But here's water at last.
> Sisters, make haste
> And slosh it down on them,
> The silly old wrecks!
>
> Sex
>
> Almighty! What they want's
> A hot bath? Send it down!
> And thou, Athenê of Athens town,
> Assist us in drowning their wheezy taunts!
>> O Trito-born! Helmet of Gold!
>> Help us to cripple their backs, the old
> Fools with their semi-incendiary brawn!

[*The* OLD MEN *capture a woman,* STRATYLLIS

STRATYLLIS:

Let me go! Let me go!

CHORAGOS ^w:

You walking corpses,
have you no shame?

CHORAGOS ^m:

I wouldn't have believed it!
An army of women in the Akropolis!

CHORAGOS ^w:

So we scare you, do we? Grandpa, you've seen
only our pickets yet!

CHORAGOS ^m:

Hey, Phaidrias!
Help me with the necks of these jabbering hens!

CHORAGOS ^w:

Down with your pots, girls! We'll need both hands
if these antiques attack us.

CHORAGOS ^m:

Want your face kicked in?

CHORAGOS ^w:

Want to try my teeth?

CHORAGOS ^m:

Look out! I've got a stick!

CHORAGOS ^w:

You lay a half-inch of your stick on Stratyllis,
and you'll never stick again!

CHORAGOS ^m:

Fall apart!

28

CHORAGOS ^w:

> I'll chew your guts!

CHORAGOS ^m:

> Euripidês! Master!

How well you knew women!

CHORAGOS ^w:

> Listen to him! Rhodippê,

up with the pots!

CHORAGOS ^m:

> Demolition of God,

what good are your pots?

CHORAGOS ^w:

> You refugee from the tomb,

what good is your fire?

CHORAGOS ^m:

> Good enough to make a pyre

to barbecue you!

CHORAGOS ^w:

> We'll squizzle your kindling!

CHORAGOS ^m:

You think so?

CHORAGOS ^w:

> Yah! Just hang around a while!

CHORAGOS ^m:

Want a touch of my torch?

CHORAGOS ^w:

> Your torch needs a bath.

CHORAGOS ^m:

How about you?

CHORAGOS ^w:

Soap for a senile bridegroom!

CHORAGOS ^m:

Senile? Hold your trap!

CHORAGOS ^w:

Just *you* try to hold it!

CHORAGOS ^m:

The yammer of women!

CHORAGOS ^w:

The yatter of men!

But you'll never sit in the jury-box again.

CHORAGOS ^m:

Gentlemen, I beg you, burn off that woman's hair!

CHORAGOS ^w:

Let it come down!

[*They empty their pots on the men*

CHORAGOS ^m:

What a way to drown!

CHORAGOS ^w:

Hot, hey?

CHORAGOS ^m:

Say,

enough!

30

CHORAGOS ^w:

          Dandruff
needs watering. I'll make you
nice and fresh.

CHORAGOS ^m:

              For God's sake, you
sluts, hold off!

SCENE I

[*Enter a* MAGISTRATE *accompanied by four constables*

MAGISTRATE:

These degenerate women! What a racket of little drums,
what a yapping for Adonis on every house-top!
It's like the time in the Assembly when I was listening
to a speech—out of order, as usual—by that fool
Demostratos, all about troops for Sicily,
that kind of nonsense—

                    and there was his wife
trotting around in circles howling
Alas for Adonis!—

              and Demostratos insisting
we must draft every last Zakynthian that can walk—
and his wife up there on the roof,
drunk as an owl, yowling
Oh weep for Adonis!—

                and that damned ox Demostratos
mooing away through the rumpus. That's what we get
for putting up with this wretched woman-business!

CHORAGOS ᵐ:

Sir, you haven't heard the half of it. They laughed at us!
Insulted us! They took pitchers of water
and nearly drowned us! We're still wringing out our clothes,
for all the world like unhousebroken brats.

MAGISTRATE:

And a good thing, by Poseidon!

35

Whose fault is it if these women-folk of ours
get out of hand? We coddle them,
we teach them to be wasteful and loose. You'll see a husband
go into a jeweler's. 'Look,' he'll say,
'jeweler,' he'll say, 'you remember that gold choker
'you made for my wife? Well, she went to a dance last night
'and broke the clasp. Now, I've got to go to Salamis,
'and can't be bothered. Run over to my house tonight,
'will you, and see if you can put it together for her.'
Or another one
goes to a cobbler—a good strong workman, too,
with an awl that was never meant for child's play. 'Here,'
he'll tell him, 'one of my wife's shoes is pinching
'her little toe. Could you come up about noon
'and stretch it out for her?'

                           Well, what do you expect?
Look at me, for example. I'm a Public Officer,
and it's one of my duties to pay off the sailors.
And where's the money? Up there in the Akropolis!
And those blasted women slam the door in my face!
But what are we waiting for?

                         —Look here, constable,
stop sniffing around for a tavern, and get us
some crowbars. We'll force their gates! As a matter of fact,
I'll do a little forcing myself.

> [*Enter* LYSISTRATA, *above, with* MYRRHINE, KALON-
> IKE, *and the* BOIOTIAN

LYSISTRATA:

No need of forcing.

Here I am, of my own accord. And all this talk
about locked doors—! We don't need locked doors,
but just the least bit of common sense.

MAGISTRATE:

Is that so, ma'am!

—Where's my constable?

—Constable,

arrest that woman, and tie her hands behind her.

LYSISTRATA:

If he touches me, I swear by Artemis
there'll be one scamp dropped from the public pay-roll tomorrow!

MAGISTRATE:

Well, constable? You're not afraid, I suppose? Grab her,
two of you, around the middle!

KALONIKE:

No, by Pándrosos!

Lay a hand on her, and I'll jump on you so hard
your guts will come out the back door!

MAGISTRATE:

That's what *you* think!

Where's the sergeant?—Here, you: tie up that trollop first,
the one with the pretty talk!

MYRRHINE:

By the Moon-Goddess!

Just you try it, and you'd better call a surgeon!

37

MAGISTRATE:

Another one!

Officer, seize that woman!

I swear

I'll put an end to this riot!

BOIOTIAN:

By the Taurian,

one inch closer and you won't have a hair on your head!

MAGISTRATE:

Lord, what a mess! And my constables seem to have left me.

But—women get the best of us? By God, no!

—Skythians!

Close ranks and forward march!

LYSISTRATA:

'Forward,' indeed!

By the Two Goddesses, what's the sense in *that*?

They're up against four companies of women

armed from top to bottom.

MAGISTRATE:

Forward, my Skythians!

LYSISTRATA:

Forward, yourselves, dear comrades!

You grainlettucebeanseedmarket girls!

You garlicandonionbreadbakery girls!

Give it to 'em! Knock 'em down! Scratch 'em!

Tell 'em what you think of 'em!

38

[*General mêlée; the Skythians yield*

        —Ah, that's enough!
Sound a retreat: good soldiers don't rob the dead!

MAGISTRATE:

A nice day *this* has been for the police!

LYSISTRATA:

Well, there you are.—Did you really think we women
would be driven like slaves? Maybe now you'll admit
that a woman knows something about glory.

MAGISTRATE:

                              Glory enough,

especially glory in bottles! Dear Lord Apollo!

CHORAGOS ^m:

Your Honor, there's no use talking to them. Words
mean nothing whatever to wild animals like these.
Think of the sousing they gave us! and the water
was not, I believe, of the purest.

CHORAGOS ^w:

You shouldn't have come after us. And if you try it again,
you'll be one eye short!—Although, as a matter of fact,
what I like best is just to stay at home and read,
like a sweet little bride: never hurting a soul, no,
never going out. But if you *must* shake hornets' nests,
look out for the hornets!

CHORUS ^m:

Good God, what can we do?   [STROPHE

What are we coming to?

These women! Who could bear it? But, for that matter, who

Will find

What they had in mind

When they seized Kranaos' city

And held it (more's the pity!)

Against us men of Athens, and our police force, too?

CHORAGOS ^m:

We might question them, I suppose. But I warn you, sir,
don't believe anything you hear! It would be un-Athenian
not to get to the bottom of this plot.

MAGISTRATE:

Very well.

My first question is this: Why, so help you God,
did you bar the gates of the Akropolis?

LYSISTRATA:

Why?

To keep the money, of course. No money, no war.

MAGISTRATE:

You think that money's the cause of war?

LYSISTRATA:

I do.

Money brought about that Peisandros business
and all the other attacks on the State. Well and good!
They'll not get another cent here!

MAGISTRATE:

And what will you do?

40

LYSISTRATA:

What a question! From now on, we intend
to control the Treasury.

MAGISTRATE:

Control the Treasury!

LYSISTRATA:

Why not? Does that seem strange? After all,
we control our household budgets.

MAGISTRATE:

But that's different!

LYSISTRATA:

'Different'? What do you mean?

MAGISTRATE:

I mean simply this:
it's the Treasury that pays for National Defense.

LYSISTRATA:

Unnecessary. We propose to abolish war!

MAGISTRATE:

Good God.—And National Security?

LYSISTRATA:

Leave that to us.

MAGISTRATE:

You?

LYSISTRATA:

Us.

MAGISTRATE:

We're done for, then!

41

LYSISTRATA:

Never mind.

We women will save you in spite of yourselves.

MAGISTRATE:

What nonsense!

LYSISTRATA:

If you like. But you must accept it, like it or not.

MAGISTRATE:

Why, this is downright subversion!

LYSISTRATA:

Maybe it is.

But we're going to save you, Judge.

MAGISTRATE:

I don't *want* to be saved!

LYSISTRATA:

Tut. The death-wish. All the more reason.

MAGISTRATE:

But the idea

of women bothering themselves about peace and war!

LYSISTRATA:

Will you listen to me?

MAGISTRATE:

Yes. But be brief, or I'll—

LYSISTRATA:

This is no time for stupid threats.

MAGISTRATE:

By the gods,

I'm losing my mind!

AN OLD WOMAN:

That's nice. If you do, remember
you've less to lose than *we* have.

MAGISTRATE:

Quiet, you old buzzard!
Now, Lysistrata: tell me what you're thinking.

LYSISTRATA:

Glad to.

Ever since this war began
we women have been watching you men, agreeing with you,
keeping our thoughts to ourselves. That doesn't mean
we were happy: we weren't, for we saw how things were going;
but we'd listen to you at dinner
arguing this way and that.

—Oh you, and your big

Top Secrets!—

And then we'd grin like little patriots
(though goodness knows we didn't feel like grinning) and ask
you:

'Dear, did the Armistice come up in Assembly today?'
And you'd say, 'None of your business! Pipe down!', you'd say.
And so we would.

AN OLD WOMAN:

I wouldn't have, by God!

MAGISTRATE:

You'd have taken a beating, then!

—Please go on.

43

LYSISTRATA:

Well, we'd be quiet. But then, you know, all at once
you men would think up something worse than ever.
Even *I* could see it was fatal. And, 'Darling,' I'd say,
'have you gone completely mad?' And my husband would look
   at me
and say, 'Wife, you've got your weaving to attend to.
'Mind your tongue, if you don't want a slap. "War's
' "a man's affair!" '

MAGISTRATE:

                Good words, and well pronounced!

LYSISTRATA:

You're a fool if you think so.

                It was hard enough
to put up with all this banquet-hall strategy.
But then we'd hear you out in the public square:
'Nobody left for the draft-quota here in Athens?'
you'd say; and, 'No,' someone else would say, 'not a man!'
And so we women decided to rescue Greece.
You might as well listen to us now: you'll have to, later.

MAGISTRATE:

You rescue Greece? Absurd!

LYSISTRATA:

                You're the absurd one!

MAGISTRATE:

You expect me to take orders from a woman?

44

LYSISTRATA:

Heavens, if that's what's bothering you, take my veil,
here, and my girdle, and my market-basket. Go home
to your weaving and your cooking! I tell you, 'War's
a woman's affair!'

CHORAGOS ^W:

Down with your pitchers, comrades,
but keep them close at hand. It's time for a rally!

CHORUS ^W:

Dance, girls, dance for peace!   [ANTISTROPHE
Who cares if our knees
Wobble and creak? Shall we not dance for such allies as these?
Their wit! their grace! their beauty!
It's a municipal duty
To dance them luck and happiness who risk their all for Greece!

CHORAGOS ^W:

Women, remember your grandmothers! Remember, you were
born
among brambles and nettles! Dance for victory!

LYSISTRATA:

O Erôs, god of delight! O Aphroditê! Kyprian!
Drench us now with the savor of love!
Let these men, getting wind of us, dream such joy
that they'll tail us through all the provinces of Hellas!

45

MAGISTRATE:

And if we do?

LYSISTRATA:

Well, for one thing, we shan't have to watch you
going to market, a spear in one hand, and heaven knows
what in the other.

CHORAGOS ᵂ:

Nicely said, by Aphroditê!

LYSISTRATA:

As things stand now, you're neither men nor women.
Armor clanking with kitchen pans and pots—
you sound like a pack of Korybantês!

MAGISTRATE:

A man must do what a man must do.

LYSISTRATA:

So I'm told.
But to see a General, complete with Gorgon-shield,
jingling along the dock to buy a couple of herrings!

CHORAGOS ᵂ:

I saw a Captain the other day—lovely fellow he was,
nice curly hair—sitting on his horse; and—can you believe it?—
he'd just bought some soup, and was pouring it into his helmet!
And there was a soldier from Thrace
swishing his lance like something out of Euripidês,
and the poor fruit-store woman got so scared
that she ran away and let him have his figs free!

46

MAGISTRATE:

All this is beside the point.

Will you be so kind
as to tell me how you mean to save Greece?

LYSISTRATA:

Of course!

Nothing could be simpler.

MAGISTRATE:

I assure you, I'm all ears.

LYSISTRATA:

Do you know anything about weaving?
Say the yarn gets tangled: we thread it
this way and that through the skein, up and down,
until it's free. And it's like that with war.
We'll send our envoys
up and down, this way and that, all over Greece,
until it's finished.

MAGISTRATE:

Yarn? Thread? Skein?
Are you out of your mind? I tell you,
war is a serious business.

LYSISTRATA:

So serious
that I'd like to go on talking about weaving.

MAGISTRATE:

All right. Go ahead.

LYSISTRATA:

The first thing we have to do
is to wash our yarn, get the dirt out of it.
You see? Isn't there too much dirt here in Athens?
You must wash those men away.

Then our spoiled wool—
that's like your job-hunters, out for a life
of no work and big pay. Back to the basket,
citizens or not, allies or not,
or friendly immigrants!

And your colonies?
Hanks of wool lost in various places. Pull them
together, weave them into one great whole,
and our voters are clothed for ever.

MAGISTRATE:

It would take a woman
to reduce state questions to a matter of carding and weaving!

LYSISTRATA:

You fool! Who were the mothers whose sons sailed off
to fight for Athens in Sicily?

MAGISTRATE:

Enough!
I beg you, do not call back those memories.

LYSISTRATA:

And then,
instead of the love that every woman needs,
we have only our single beds, where we can dream
of our husbands off with the Army.

48

                              Bad enough for wives!
But what about our girls, getting older every day,
and older, and no kisses?

MAGISTRATE:

                         Men get older, too.

LYSISTRATA:

Not in the same sense.

                    A soldier's discharged,
and he may be bald and toothless, yet he'll find
a pretty young thing to go to bed with.

                                   But a woman!
Her beauty is gone with the first grey hair.
She can spend her time
consulting the oracles and the fortune-tellers,
but they'll never send her a husband.

MAGISTRATE:

Still, if a man can rise to the occasion—

LYSISTRATA:

Rise? Rise, yourself!

                              [*Furiously*

Go invest in a coffin!
                    You've money enough.
                                   I'll bake you
a cake for the Underworld.
                    And here's your funeral
wreath!

                              [*She pours water upon him*

49

MYRRHINE:

And here's another!

[More water

KALONIKE:

And here's
my contribution!

[More water

LYSISTRATA:

What are you waiting for?
All aboard *Styx* Ferry!

Charôn's calling for you!
It's sailing-time: don't disrupt the schedule!

MAGISTRATE:

The insolence of women! And to me!
No, by God, I'll go back to court and show
the rest of the Bench the things that might happen to them!

[Exit MAGISTRATE

LYSISTRATA:

Really, I suppose we should have laid out his corpse
on the doorstep, in the usual way.

But never mind!
We'll give him the rites of the dead tomorrow morning!

[Exit LYSISTRATA *with* MYRRHINE *and* KALONIKE

CHORAL EPISODE

CHORUS ^m: [STROPHE 1

Sons of Liberty, strip off your clothes for action! Men, arise!

Shall we stand here limp and useless while old Kleisthenês' allies

Prod a herd of furious grandmas to attempt to bring to pass

A female restoration of the Reign of Hippias?

Forbid it, gods misogynist!

Return our Treasury, at least!

We must clothe ourselves and feed ourselves to face these civic
rages,

And who can do a single thing if they cut off our wages?

CHORAGOS ^m:

Gentlemen, we are disgraced forever if we allow

these madwomen to jabber about spears and shields

and make friends with the Spartans. What's a Spartan? a wild

wolf's a safer companion any day! No; their plan's

to bring back Dictatorship; and we won't stand for that!

From now on, let's go armed, each one of us

a new Aristogeiton!

And to begin with,

I propose to poke a number of teeth

down the gullet of that harridan over there.

CHORUS ^w: [ANTISTROPHE 1

Hold your tongues, you senile bravoes, or, I swear, when you get
home

Your own mothers wouldn't know you! Strip for action, ladies,
come!

53

I bore the holy vessels in my eighth year, and at ten
I was pounding out the barley for Athenê Goddess; then
                    They elected me Little Bear
                    For Artemis at Brauron Fair;
I'd been made a Basket-Carrier by the time I came of age:
So trust me to advise you in this feminist rampage!

CHORAGOS ^w:

As a woman, I pay my taxes to the State,
though I pay them in baby boys. What do you contribute,
you impotent horrors? Nothing but waste:
our treasury, the so-called Glory of the Persian Wars,
gone! rifled! parceled out for privilege! And you
have the insolence to control public policy,
leading us all to disaster!
                              No, don't answer back
unless you want the heel of my slipper
slap against that ugly jaw of yours!

CHORUS ^m:

                    What impudence!   [STROPHE 2
                    What malevolence!
                    Comrades, make haste,
All those of you who still are sensitive below the waist!
                    Off with your clothes, men!
                    Nobody knows when
                        We'll put them back on.

54

Remember Leipsydrion!
We may be old,
But let's be bold!

CHORAGOS ^m:

Give them an inch, and we're done for! We'll have them
launching boats next and planning naval strategy.
Or perhaps they fancy themselves as cavalry!
That's fair enough: women know how to ride,
they're good in the saddle. Just think of Mikôn's paintings,
all those Amazons wrestling with men! No, it's time
to bridle these wild mares!

CHORUS ^w:

    Hold on, or   [ANTISTROPHE 2
    You *are* done for,
    By the Two Goddesses above!
Strip, strip, my women: we've got the veterans on the move!
    Tangle with me, Gramps,
    And you'll have cramps
      For the rest of your days!
      No more beans! No more cheese!
    My two legs
    Will scramble your eggs!

CHORAGOS ^w:

If Lampitô stands by me, and that elegant

55

Theban girl, Ismenia—what good are *you*?

Pass your laws!
Laws upon laws, you decrepit legislators!
At the worst you're just a nuisance, rationing Boiotian eels
on the Feast of Hekatê, making our girls go without!
That was statesmanship! And we'll have to put up with it
until some patriot slits your silly old gizzards!

[*Exeunt omnes*

SCENE II

[*The scene shifts to a court within the Akropolis.*
Re-enter LYSISTRATA

CHORAGOS ^W:

But Lysistrata! Leader! Why such a grim face?

LYSISTRATA:

Oh the behavior of these idiotic women!
There's something about the female temperament
that I can't bear!

CHORAGOS ^W:

What in the world do you mean?

LYSISTRATA:

Exactly what I say.

CHORAGOS ^W:

What dreadful thing has happened?
Come, tell us: we're all your friends.

LYSISTRATA:

It isn't easy
to say it; yet, God knows, we can't hush it up.

CHORAGOS ^W:

Well, then? Out with it!

LYSISTRATA:

To put it bluntly,
we're desperate for men.

CHORAGOS ^W:

Almighty God!

LYSISTRATA:

Why bring God into it?—No, it's just as I say.

59

I can't manage them any longer: they've gone man-crazy,
they're all trying to get out.

                        Why, look:
one of them was sneaking out the back door
over there by Pan's cave; another
was sliding down the walls with rope and tackle;
another was climbing aboard a sparrow, ready to take off
for the nearest brothel—I dragged *her* back by the hair!
They're all finding some reason to leave.

                                    Look there!
There goes another one.

                        —Just a minute, you!
Where are you off to so fast?

FIRST WOMAN:

                            I've got to get home!
I've a lot of Milesian wool, and the worms are spoiling it.

LYSISTRATA:

Oh bother you and your worms! Get back inside!

FIRST WOMAN:

I'll be back right away, I swear I will!

I just want to get it stretched out on my bed.

LYSISTRATA:

You'll do no such thing. You'll stay right here.

FIRST WOMAN:

                            And my wool?

You want it ruined?

60

LYSISTRATA:

Yes, for all I care.

SECOND WOMAN:

Oh dear! My lovely new flax from Amorgos—
I left it at home, all uncarded!

LYSISTRATA:

Another one!

And all she wants is someone to card her flax.
Get back in there!

SECOND WOMAN:

But I swear by the Moon-Goddess,

the minute I get it done, I'll be back!

LYSISTRATA:

I say No!

If you, why not all the other women as well?

THIRD WOMAN:

O Lady Eileithyia! Radiant goddess! Thou
intercessor for women in childbirth! Stay, I pray thee,
oh stay this parturition! Shall I pollute
a sacred spot?

LYSISTRATA:

And what's the matter with *you*?

THIRD WOMAN:

I'm having a baby—any minute now!

LYSISTRATA:

But you weren't pregnant yesterday.

61

THIRD WOMAN:

Well, I am today!

Let me go home for a midwife, Lysistrata:
there's not much time.

LYSISTRATA:

I never heard such nonsense.

What's that bulging under your cloak?

THIRD WOMAN:

A little baby boy.

LYSISTRATA:

It certainly isn't. But it's something hollow,
like a basin or— Why, it's the helmet of Athenê!
And you said you were having a baby!

THIRD WOMAN:

Well, I am! So there!

LYSISTRATA:

Then why the helmet?

THIRD WOMAN:

I was afraid that my pains
might begin here in the Akropolis; and I wanted
to drop my chick into it, just as the dear doves do.

LYSISTRATA:

Lies! Evasions!—But at least one thing's clear:
you can't leave the place before your purification.

THIRD WOMAN:

But I can't stay here in the Akropolis! Last night I dreamed
of a snake.

62

FIRST WOMAN:

> And those horrible owls, the noise they make!
> I can't get a bit of sleep; I'm just about dead.

LYSISTRATA:

You useless girls, that's enough: Let's have no more lying.
Of course you want your men. But don't you imagine
that they want you just as much? I'll give you my word,
their nights must be pretty hard.

> Just stick it out!

A little patience, that's all, and our battle's won.
I have heard an Oracle. Should you like to hear it?

FIRST WOMAN:

An Oracle? Yes, tell us!

LYSISTRATA:

> Quiet, then.—Here

is what it said:

IF EVER THE SWALLOWS, ESCHEWING HOOPOE-
    BIRDS,
SHALL CONSPIRE TOGETHER TO DENY THEM ALL
    ACCESS,
THEIR GRIEF IS FOREVER OVER.

> These are the words

from the Shrine itself.

> AYE, AND ZEUS WILL REDRESS

THEIR WRONGS, AND SET THE LOWER ABOVE
    THE HIGHER.

FIRST WOMAN:

Does that mean we'll be on top?

LYSISTRATA:

BUT IF THEY RETIRE,
EACH SWALLOW HER OWN WAY, FROM THIS
    HOLY PLACE,
LET THE WORLD PROCLAIM NO BIRD OF SORRIER
    GRACE
THAN THE SWALLOW.

FIRST WOMAN:

I swear, *that* Oracle makes sense!

LYSISTRATA:

Now, then, by all the gods,
let's show that we're bigger than these annoyances.
Back to your places! Let's not disgrace the Oracle.

> [*Exeunt* LYSISTRATA *and the dissident women; the* CHORUSES *renew their conflict.*

CHORAL EPISODE

CHORUS ^m:

I know a little story that I learned way back in school
Goes like this:
Once upon a time there was a young man—and no fool—
Named Melanion; and his
One aversi-on was marriage. He loathed the very thought!
So he ran off to the hills, and in a special grot
Raised a dog, and spent his days
Hunting rabbits. And it says
That he never never never did come home.
It might be called a refuge *from* the womb.
All right,
         all right,
                  all right!
We're as pure as young Melanion, and we hate the very sight
Of you sluts!

A MAN:

How about a kiss, old woman?

A WOMAN:

Here's an onion in your eye!

A MAN:

A kick in the guts, then?

A WOMAN:

Try, old bristle-tail, just try!

A MAN:

Yet they say Myronidês

On hands and knees
Looked just as shaggy fore and aft as I!

CHORUS ^w: [ANTISTROPHE

Well, *I* know a little story, and it's just as good as yours.
Goes like this:
Once there was a man named Timon—a rough diamond, of
    course,
And that whiskery face of his
Looked like murder in the shrubbery. By God, he was a son
Of the Furies, let me tell you! And what did he do but run
From the world and all its ways,
Cursing mankind! And it says
That his choicest execrations as of then
Were leveled almost wholly at *old* men.
All right,
       all right,
          all right!
But there's one thing about Timon: he could always stand the
    sight
Of us 'sluts'!

A WOMAN:

How about a crack in the jaw, Pop?

A MAN:

I can take it, Ma—no fear!

A WOMAN:

How about a kick in the face?

68

A MAN:

You'd show your venerable rear.

A WOMAN:

I may be old;

But I've been told

That I've nothing to worry about down there!

SCENE III

[*Re-enter* LYSISTRATA

LYSISTRATA:

Oh, quick, girls, quick! Come here!

CHORAGOS ^w:

What is it?

LYSISTRATA:

A man!

A man simply bulging with love!

O Kyprian Queen,

O Paphian, O Kythereian! Hear us and aid us!

CHORAGOS ^w:

Where is this enemy?

LYSISTRATA:

Over there, by Deméter's shrine.

CHORAGOS ^w:

Damned if he isn't. But who *is* he?

MYRRHINE:

My husband.

Kinesias.

LYSISTRATA:

Oh then, get busy! Tease him! Undermine him!
Wreck him! Give him everything—kissing, tickling, nudging,
whatever you generally torture him with—: give him everything
except what we swore on the wine we would not give.

MYRRHINE:

Trust me!

73

LYSISTRATA:

    I do. But I'll help you get him started.
The rest of you women, stay back.

                              [*Enter* KINESIAS

KINESIAS:

                      Oh God! Oh my God!
I'm stiff for lack of exercise. All I can do to stand up!

LYSISTRATA:

Halt! Who are you, approaching our lines?

KINESIAS:

                        Me? I.

LYSISTRATA:

A man?

KINESIAS:

    You have eyes, haven't you?

LYSISTRATA:

                      Go away.

KINESIAS:

Who says so?

LYSISTRATA:

    Officer of the Day.

KINESIAS:

                    Officer, I beg you,
by all the gods at once, bring Myrrhinê out!

LYSISTRATA:

Myrrhinê? And who, my good sir, are you?

74

KINESIAS:

Kinesias. Last name's Pennison. Her husband.

LYSISTRATA:

Oh, of course. I beg your pardon. We're glad to see you.
We've heard so much about you. Dearest Myrrhinê
is always talking about 'Kinesias'—never nibbles an egg
or an apple without saying
'Here's to Kinesias!'

KINESIAS:

Do you really mean it?

LYSISTRATA:

I do.

When we're discussing men, she always says,
'Well, after all, there's nobody like Kinesias!'

KINESIAS:

Good God.—Well, then, please send her down here.

LYSISTRATA:

And what do *I* get out of it?

KINESIAS:

A standing promise.

LYSISTRATA:

I'll take it up with her.

[*Exit* LYSISTRATA

KINESIAS:

But be quick about it!
Lord, what's life without a wife? Can't eat. Can't sleep.

Every time I go home, the place is so empty, so
insufferably sad! Love's killing me! Oh,
hurry!

> [*Enter* MANES, *a slave, with Kinesias' baby; the voice
> of* MYRRHINE *is heard off-stage.*

MYRRHINE:

> But of course I love him! Adore him!—But no,
he hates love. No. I won't go down.

> [*Enter* MYRRHINE, *above*

KINESIAS:

> Myrrhinê!
Darlingest little Myrrhinê! Come down quick!

MYRRHINE:

> Certainly not.

KINESIAS:

> Not? But why, Myrrhinê?

MYRRHINE:

> Why? You don't need me.

KINESIAS:

> Need you? My God, *look* at me!

MYRRHINE:

> So long!

> [*Turns to go*

KINESIAS:

> Myrrhinê, Myrrhinê, Myrrhinê!

76

If not for my sake, for our child!

                               [Pinches BABY

                  —All right, you: pipe up!

BABY:

Mummie! Mummie! Mummie!

KINESIAS:

                  You hear that?

Pitiful, I call it. Six days now
with never a bath; no food; enough to break your heart!

MYRRHINE:

My darlingest child! What a father *you* acquired!

KINESIAS:

At least come down for his sake!

MYRRHINE:

                  I suppose I must.

Oh, this mother business!

                                     [Exit

KINESIAS:

           How pretty she is! And younger!
She's so much nicer when she's bothered!

                    [MYRRHINE *enters, below*

MYRRHINE:

                  Dearest child,
you're as sweet as your father's horrid. Give me a kiss.

                77

KINESIAS:

Now you see how wrong it was to get involved
in this scheming League of women. All this agony
for nothing!

MYRRHINE:

Keep your hands to yourself!

KINESIAS:

But our house
going to rack and ruin?

MYRRHINE:

I don't care.

KINESIAS:

And your knitting
all torn to pieces by the chickens? Don't you care?

MYRRHINE:

Not at all.

KINESIAS:

And our vows to Aphroditê?
Oh, *won't* you come back?

MYRRHINE:

No.—At least, not until you men
make a treaty to end the war.

KINESIAS:

Why, if that's all you want,
by God, we'll make your treaty!

MYRRHINE:

Oh? Very well.

78

When you've done that, I'll come home. But meanwhile,
I've sworn an oath.

KINESIAS:

> Don't worry.—Now, let's have fun.

MYRRHINE:

No! Stop it! I said no!

> —Although, of course,

I *do* love you.

KINESIAS:

> I know you do. Darling Myrrhinê:

come, shall we?

MYRRHINE:

> Are you out of your mind? In front of the child?

KINESIAS:

Take him home, Manês.

> [*Exit* MANES *with baby*

> There. He's gone.

> > Come on!

There's nothing to stop us now.

MYRRHINE:

> You devil! But where?

KINESIAS:

In Pan's cave. What could be snugger than that?

MYRRHINE:

But my purification before I go back to the Citadel?

KINESIAS:

There's always the Klepsydra.

MYRRHINE:

                    And my oath?

KINESIAS:

                         Leave the oath to me.

After all, I'm the man.

MYRRHINE:

                Well . . . if you say so!

                     I'll go find a bed.

KINESIAS:

Oh, bother a bed! The ground's good enough for me!

MYRRHINE:

No. You're a bad man, but you deserve something better than
dirt.

                     [*Exit* MYRRHINE

KINESIAS:

What a love she is! And how thoughtful!

               [*Re-enter* MYRRHINE

MYRRHINE:

                    Here's your bed.

Now let me get my clothes off.

               But, good horrors!

We haven't a mattress!

KINESIAS:

            Oh, forget the mattress!

MYRRHINE:

                                        No.

Just lying on blankets? Too sordid!

KINESIAS:

                              Give me a kiss.

MYRRHINE:

Just a second.

                              [*Exit* MYRRHINE

KINESIAS:

              I swear, I'll explode!

                              [*Re-enter* MYRRHINE

MYRRHINE:

                        Here's your mattress.
Go to bed now. I'll just take my dress off.

                              But look—

where's our pillow?

KINESIAS:

              I don't need a pillow!

MYRRHINE:

                        Well, *I* do.

                              [*Exit* MYRRHINE

KINESIAS:

I don't suppose even Heraklês
would stand for this!

                              [*Re-enter* MYRRHINE

MYRRHINE:

There we are. Ups-a-daisy!

KINESIAS:

So we are. Well, come to bed.

MYRRHINE:

But I wonder:

is everything ready now?

KINESIAS:

I can swear to that. Come, darling!

MYRRHINE:

Just getting out of my girdle.

But remember, now,

what you promised about the treaty!

KINESIAS:

I'll remember.

MYRRHINE:

But no coverlet!

KINESIAS:

Damn it, I'll be

your coverlet!

MYRRHINE:

Be right back.

[*Exit* MYRRHINE

KINESIAS:

This girl and her coverlets

will be the death of me.

[*Re-enter* MYRRHINE

82

MYRRHINE:

Here we are. Up you go!

KINESIAS:

Up? I've been up for ages!

MYRRHINE:

Some perfume?

KINESIAS:

No, by Apollo!

MYRRHINE:

Yes, by Aphroditê!
I don't care whether you want it or not.

[*Exit* MYRRHINE

KINESIAS:

For love's sake, hurry!

[*Re-enter* MYRRHINE

MYRRHINE:

Here, in your hand. Rub it right in.

KINESIAS:

Never cared for perfume.
And this is particularly strong. Still, here goes!

MYRRHINE:

What a nitwit I am! I brought you the Rhodian bottle!

KINESIAS:

Forget it.

MYRRHINE:

No trouble at all. You just wait here.

[*Exit* MYRRHINE

KINESIAS:

God damn the man who invented perfume!

[*Re-enter* MYRRHINE

MYRRHINE:

At last! The right bottle!

KINESIAS:

I've got the rightest
bottle of all, and it's right here waiting for you.
Darling, forget everything else. Do come to bed!

MYRRHINE:

Just let me get my shoes off.

—And, by the way,
you'll vote for the treaty?

KINESIAS:

I'll think about it.

[MYRRHINE *runs away*

There! That's done it! Off she runs,
with never a thought for the way I'm feeling. I must
have *some*one, or I'll go mad! Myrrhinê
has just about ruined me.

And you, strutting little soldier:

84

what about you? There's nothing for it, I guess,
but an expedition to old Dog-fox's bordello.

CHORUS ^m:

> She's left you in a sorry state:
> You have my sympathy.
> What upright citizen could bear
> Your pain? I swear, not I!
> Just the look of you, with never a woman
> To come to your aid! It isn't human!

KINESIAS:

> The agony!

CHORAGOS ^m:

> Well, why not?
> She has you on the spot!

CHORAGOS ^w:

A lovelier girl never breathed, you old sot!

KINESIAS:

> A lovelier girl? Zeus! Zeus!
> Produce a hurricane
> To hoist these lovely girls aloft
> And drop them down again
> Bump on our lances! Then they'd know
> What they do that makes men suffer so.

[*Exit* KINESIAS

85

SCENE IV

[*Enter a* SPARTAN HERALD

HERALD:

Gentlemen, Ah beg you will be so kind
as to direct me to the Central Committee.
Ah have a communication.

[*Re-enter* MAGISTRATE

MAGISTRATE:

       Are you a man,

or a fertility symbol?

HERALD:

      Ah refuse to answer that question!
Ah'm a certified herald from Spahta, and Ah've come
to talk about an ahmistice.

MAGISTRATE:

       Then why

that spear under your cloak?

HERALD:

      Ah have no speah!

MAGISTRATE:

You don't walk naturally, with your tunic
poked out so. You have a tumor, maybe,
or a hernia?

HERALD:

   No, by Kastor!

MAGISTRATE:

      Well,

something's wrong, I can see that. And I don't like it.

HERALD:

Colonel, Ah resent this.

MAGISTRATE:

So I see. But what *is* it?

HERALD:

A scroll

with a message from Spahta.

MAGISTRATE:

Oh. I've heard about these scrolls.

Well, then, man, speak out: How are things in Sparta?

HERALD:

Hard, Colonel, hard! We're at a standstill.

Can't seem to think of anything but women.

MAGISTRATE:

How curious! Tell me, do you Spartans think

that maybe Pan's to blame?

HERALD:

Pan? No. Lampitô and her little naked friends.

They won't let a man come near them.

MAGISTRATE:

How are you handling it?

HERALD:

Losing our minds,

if you want to know, and walking around hunched over

like men carrying candles in a gale.

90

The women have sworn they'll have nothing to do with us
until we get a treaty.

MAGISTRATE:

Yes. I know.

It's a general uprising, sir, in all parts of Greece.
But as for the answer—

Sir: go back to Sparta
and have them send us your Armistice Commission.
I'll arrange things in Athens.

And I may say
that my standing is good enough to make them listen.

HERALD:

A man after mah own heart! Sir, Ah thank you!

[*Exit* HERALD

CHORAL EPISODE

CHORUS ^m:

> Oh these women! Where will you find   [STROPHE
> A slavering beast that's more unkind?
> > Where a hotter fire?
> Give me a panther, any day!
> He's not so merciless as they,
> > And panthers don't conspire!

CHORUS ^w:

> We may be hard, you silly old ass,   [ANTISTROPHE
> But who brought you to this stupid pass?
> > You're the ones to blame.
> Fighting with us, your oldest friends,
> Simply to serve your selfish ends—
> > Really, you have no shame!

CHORAGOS ^m:

No, I'm through with women for ever!

CHORAGOS ^w:

> > > > > If you say so.

Still, you might put some clothes on. You look too absurd
standing around naked. Come, get into this cloak.

CHORAGOS ^m:

Thank you; you're right. I merely took it off
because I was in such a temper.

CHORAGOS ^w:

> > > > That's much better

Now you resemble a man again.

Why have you been so horrid?
And look: there's some sort of insect in your eye!
Shall I take it out?

CHORAGOS ᵐ:

An insect, is it? So that's
what's been bothering me! Lord, yes: take it out!

CHORAGOS ʷ:

You might be more polite.

—But, heavens!
What an enormous gnat!

CHORAGOS ᵐ:

You've saved my life.
That gnat was drilling an artesian well
in my left eye.

CHORAGOS ʷ:

Let me wipe
those tears away!—And now: one little kiss?

CHORAGOS ᵐ:

Over my dead body!

CHORAGOS ʷ:

You're so difficult!

CHORAGOS ᵐ:

These impossible women! How they do get around us!
The poet was right: Can't live with them, or without them!
But let's be friends.

And to celebrate, you might lead off with an Ode.

96

CHORUS ^W:

Let it never be said   [STROPHE

That my tongue is malicious:

Both by word and by deed

I would set an example that's noble and gracious.

We've had sorrow and care

Till we're sick of the tune.

Is there anyone here

Who would like a small loan?

My purse is crammed,

As you'll soon find;

And you needn't pay me back if the Peace gets signed!

I've invited to lunch

Some Karystian rips—

An esurient bunch,

But I've ordered a menu to water their lips!

I can still make soup

And slaughter a pig.

You're all coming, I hope?

But a bath first, I beg!

Walk right up

As though you owned the place,

And you'll get the front door slammed to in your face!

SCENE V

[*Enter* SPARTAN AMBASSADOR, *with entourage*

CHORAGOS ^m:

The Commission has arrived from Sparta.

How oddly

they're walking!

Gentlemen, welcome to Athens!

How is life in Lakonia?

AMBASSADOR:

Need we discuss that?

Simply use your eyes.

CHORUS ^m:

The poor man's right:

What a sight!

AMBASSADOR:

Words fail me.

But come, gentlemen, call in your Commissioners,
and let's get down to a Peace.

CHORAGOS ^m:

The state we're in! Can't bear

a stitch below the waist. It's a kind of pelvic

paralysis.

AN ATHENIAN:

Won't somebody call Lysistrata?

She has the answer.

A SPARTAN:

Yes, there, look at him.

Same thing.

Seh, do y'all feel a certain strain
early in the morning?

ATHENIAN:

I do, sir. It's worse than a strain.
A few more days, and there's nothing for us but Kleisthenês,
that broken blossom!

CHORAGOS ^m:

But you'd better get dressed again.
You know these prudes who go around Athens with chisels,
looking for prominent statues.

ATHENIAN:

Sir, you are right.

SPARTAN:

He certainly is! Ah'll put mah own clothes back on.

[*Enter* ATHENIAN COMMISSIONERS

AN ATHENIAN:

They're no better off than we are!

—Greetings, Lakonians!

SPARTAN: [*To one of his own group:*

Colonel, we got dressed just in time. Ah sweah,
if they'd seen us the way we were, there'd have been a new war
between the states.

ATHENIAN:

Call the meeting to order.

Now, Lakonians,

what's your proposal?

AMBASSADOR:

We'd lahk to consider peace.

ATHENIAN:

Good. That's on our minds, too.

—Summon Lysistrata.

We'll never get anywhere without her.

AMBASSADOR:

Lysistrata?

Summon Lysis-*any*body! Only, summon!

CHORAGOS ᵐ:

No need to summon:

here she is, herself.

[*Enter* LYSISTRATA

Lysistrata! Lion of women!
This is your hour to be
hard and yielding, outspoken and sly, austere and
gentle. You see here
the best brains of Hellas (confused, I admit,
by your devious charming) met as one man
to turn the future over to you.

LYSISTRATA:

That's fair enough,

unless you men take it into your heads
to turn to each other instead of to me. But I'd know

103

soon enough if you did!

                   —Where is that goddess of Peace?
Go, some of you: bring her here.

                           [*Exeunt two* SERVANTS

               And now,
summon the Spartan Commission. Treat them courteously:
our husbands have been lax in that respect.
Take them by the hand, women,
or by anything else, if they seem unwilling.

                         —Spartans:
you stand here. Athenians: on this side. Now listen to me.

       [*Re-enter* SERVANTS, *staggering under the weight of
       a more than life-size statue of a naked woman: this
       is* PEACE.

I'm only a woman, I know; but I've a mind,
and I can distinguish between sense and foolishness.
I owe the first to my father; the rest
to the local politicians. So much for that.
Now, then.
What I have to say concerns both sides in this war.
We are all Greeks.
Must I remind you of Thermopylai? of Olympia?
of Delphoi? names deep in all our hearts?
And yet you men go raiding through the country,
Greek killing Greek, storming down Greek cities—

                      104

and all the time the Barbarian across the sea
is waiting for his chance.—That's my first point.

AN ATHENIAN:

Lord! I can hardly contain myself!

LYSISTRATA:

And you Spartans:

Was it so long ago that Perikleidês
came here to beg our help? I can see him still,
his white face, his sombre gown. And what did he want?
An army from Athens! Messenia
was at your heels, and the sea-god splitting your shores.
Well, Kimôn and his men,
four thousand infantry, marched out of here to save you.
What thanks do we get? You come back to murder us.

ATHENIAN:

Can't trust a Spartan, Lysistrata!

A SPARTAN:

Ah admit it.

When Ah look at those legs, Ah sweah Ah can't trust mahself!

LYSISTRATA:

And you, men of Athens:
you might remember that bad time when we were down,
and an army came from Sparta
and sent Hippias and the Thessalians
whimpering back to the hills. That was Sparta,
and only Sparta; without Sparta, we'd now be
cringing helots, not walking about like free men!

[*From this point, the male responses are less to* LY-
SISTRATA *than to the statue of* PEACE.

A SPARTAN:

An eloquent speech!

AN ATHENIAN:

An elegant construction!

LYSISTRATA:

Why are we fighting each other? Why not make peace?

AMBASSADOR:

Spahta is ready, ma'am,

so long as we get that place back.

LYSISTRATA:

Place? What place?

AMBASSADOR:

Ah refer to Pylos.

MAGISTRATE:

Not while I'm alive, by God!

LYSISTRATA:

You'd better give in.

MAGISTRATE:

But—what were we fighting about?

LYSISTRATA:

Lots of places left.

MAGISTRATE:

All right. Well, then:

Hog Island first, and that gulf behind there, and the land between

the Legs of Megara.

106

AMBASSADOR:

Mah government objects.

LYSISTRATA:

Over-ruled. Why fuss about a pair of legs?

[*General assent; the statue of* PEACE *is removed*

AN ATHENIAN:

Let's take off our clothes and plow our fields.

A SPARTAN:

Ah'll fertilize mahn first, by the Heavenly Twins!

LYSISTRATA:

And so you shall,

once we have peace. If you are serious,

go, both of you, and talk with your allies.

ATHENIAN:

Too much talk already. We'll stand together!

We've only one end in view. All that we want

is our women: and I speak for our allies.

AMBASSADOR:

Mah government concurs.

ATHENIAN:

So does Karystos.

LYSISTRATA:

Good.—But before you come inside

to join your wives at supper, you must perform

the usual lustration. Then we'll open

our baskets for you, and all that we have is yours.

But you must promise upright good behavior
from this day on. Then each man home with his woman!

ATHENIAN:

Let's get it over with!

SPARTAN:

Lead on: Ah follow!

ATHENIAN:

Quick as a cat can wink!

[*Exeunt all but the* CHORUSES

CHORUS ᵂ:

Embroideries ánd   [ANTISTROPHE
Twinkling ornaments ánd
Pretty dresses—I hand
Them all over to you, and with never a qualm.
They'll be nice for your daughters
On festival days
When the girls bring the Goddess
The ritual prize.
Come in, one and all:
Take what you will.
I've nothing here so tightly corked that you can't make it spill!

You may search my house,
But you'll not find
The least thing of use,

Unless your two eyes are keener than mine.

Your numberless brats

Are half starved? and your slaves?

Courage, grandpa! I've lots

Of grain left, and big loaves.

I'll fill your guts,

I'll go the whole hog;

But if you come too close to me, remember: 'ware the dog!

[*Exeunt* CHORUSES

ÉXODOS

[*An* ATHENIAN DRUNKARD *approaches the gate and is
halted by a* SENTRY

DRUNKARD:

Open. The. Door.

SENTRY:

Now, friend, just shove along!
So you want to sit down! If it weren't such an old joke,
I'd tickle your tail with this torch. Just the sort of thing
that this kind of audience appreciates.

DRUNKARD:

I. Stay. Right. Here.

SENTRY:

Oh, all right. But you'll see some funny sights!

DRUNKARD:

Bring. Them. On.

SENTRY:

No, what am I thinking of?
The gentlemen from Sparta are just coming back from supper.
Get out of here, or I'll scalp you!

[*Exit* DRUNKARD; *the general company re-enters; the
two* CHORUSES *now represent* SPARTANS *and* ATHE-
NIANS.

MAGISTRATE:

I must say,
I've never tasted a better meal. And those Lakonians!
They're gentlemen, by the Lord! Just goes to show:

a drink to the wise is sufficient. And why not?
A sober man's an ass.
Men of Athens, mark my words: the only efficient
Ambassador's a drunk Ambassador. Is that clear?
Look: we go to Sparta,
and when we get there we're dead sober. The result?
Everyone cackling at everyone else. They make speeches;
and even if we understand, we get it all wrong
when we file our reports in Athens. But today—!
Everybody's happy. Couldn't tell the difference
between *Drink to Me Only* and
the *Star Spangled Athens*.

What's a few lies,
washed down in good strong drink?

[Re-enter DRUNKARD

SENTRY:

God almighty,
he's back again!

DRUNKARD:

I. Resume. My. Place.

A SPARTAN: *[To an* ATHENIAN:
I beg you, seh,
take your instrument in your hand and play for us.
Ah'm told
you understand the in*tri*cacies of the floot?
Ah'd lahk to execute a song and dance

114

in honor of Athens,

        and, of course, of Spahta.

     [*The following song is a solo—an aria—accompanied by the flute. The* CHORUS OF SPARTANS *begins a slow dance.*

DRUNKARD:

Toot. On. Your. Flute.

CHORAGOS [s]:

     Mnemosynê,

     Inspire once more the Grecian Muse

     To sing of glory glory glory without end.

     Sing Artemesion's shore,

     Where Athens fluttered the Persian fleet—

     Alalaí, that great

     Victory! Sing Leonidas and his men,

     Those wild boars, sweat and blood

     Down in a red drench. Then, then

     The barbarians broke, though they had stood

     A myriad strong before!

               O Artemis,

     Virgin Goddess, whose darts

     Flash in our forests: approve

     This pact of peace, and join our hearts,

     From this day on, in love.

     Huntress, descend!

LYSISTRATA:

All that will come in time.

But now, Lakonians,
take home your wives. Athenians, take yours.
Each man be kind to his woman; and you, women,
be equally kind. Never again, pray God,
shall we lose our way in such madness.

—And now
let's dance our joy!

[*From this point the dance becomes general*

CHORUS OF ATHENIANS:

Dance!

Dance!

Dance, you Graces!
Artemis, dance!

Dance, Phoibos, Lord of dancing!
Dance, Dionysos, in a scurry of Maenads!

Dance, Zeus Thunderer!

Dance, Lady Herê,
Queen of the Sky!

Dance, dance, all you gods!
Dance for the dearest, the bringer of peace,
Deathless Aphroditê!

LYSISTRATA:

Now let us have another song from Sparta.

116

CHORUS OF SPARTANS:

From Taÿgetos' skyey summit,
Lakonian Muse, come down!
Sing the glories of Apollo,
Regent of Amyklai Town.
Sing of Leda's Twins,
Those gallant sons,
On the banks of Eurotas—
Alalaí Evohé!

Here's to our girls
With their tangling curls,
Legs a-wriggle,
Bellies a-jiggle,
A riot of hair,
A fury of feet,
Evohé! Evohaí! Evohé!
as they pass
Dancing,
dancing,
dancing,
to greet
Athenê of the House of Brass!

117

NOTES
AND
INDEX OF PROPER NAMES

When is a note not a note, but an impertinence? Faced with the necessity of choosing between all or nothing, I have chosen all; and I apologize to the reader who may be offended by finding himself provided with an identification of Zeus, or of Athens, or of some other commonplace. My experience has been that, like Miss Millay's islands, there are no commonplaces any more; none, at any rate, that can be trusted. A man who has been informed, as I have been by a student of average intelligence, that Pontius Pilate was one of the Four Evangelists—no; you are my *Lectores Benevoli,* and I am sure that you will understand this poem; but I will not trust even 'Athens' to you without a Note.

DF

NOTES

Page

5: *those heavenly eels:* See note on BOIOTIA.

8: *that dance of abs:* Athenian girls were brought up in seclusion. In Sparta, however, girls were expected to participate in athletic exercises. The 'dance' referred to here is the strenuous *bibasis,* in which the executant must strike her buttocks with her heels.

8: *Lawdy:* She swears 'by the Two,' which, in Sparta, meant the Heavenly Twins, Kastor and Polydeukês. The Athenian 'by the Two' was reserved to women only, and referred to Demêter and Persephoneia.

10: *that General:* His name was Eukratês, and Σ * describes him as 'an Athenian general, for sale, a traitor, and a mercenary'; but Σ seems to be as much in the dark as we, when it comes to identifying him.

11: *drink up the proceeds:* The Athenian women were frequently satirized as being heavy drinkers.—The joke here, such as it is, depends upon a rhetorical trope by which the expected conclusion of a sentence is twisted into an unexpected incongruity. Thus, one would have expected Myrrhinê to say that she would pawn her best dress and contribute the proceeds to the Cause.

13: *when he saw Helen's breast:* An allusion to Euripides' *Andromachê,* 627, *sqq;* where Menelaos, about to stab his faithless wife, is overcome by her beauty and drops his sword.

15: *there's lots of money . . . in the Akropolis:* An enormous sum set

* Σ = Scholiast.

121

aside by Perikles at the beginning of the War, for use in an emergency.

15: *Where's our Inner Guard?:* See note on SKYTHIANS.

16: *Why not a white horse?:* Obscure; and a field-day for the commentators. Σ rightly observes that 'the horse' is a schema of coitus, but he also remarks that the Amazones (see note on MIKON) were accustomed to sacrifice white horses. According to Herodotos, the Amazones, furious horsewomen, were noted for their white (we should say 'ash-blonde') hair. I should like to find here a reference to a forgotten notable named Leukippos ('White Horse')—certainly not the philosopher, but possibly a general in disrepute. No trace, however.

23: *the sacred statuar-y:* The august statue of Athenê Polias, which fell from Heaven upon the Akropolis.

27: *O Trito-born!:* Name for Athenê, who, according to some accounts, was born near Lake Tritonis, in Libya.

28: *Stratyllis:* The text—or, rather, the authority of the texts—is confused here. According to some, Stratyllis is the Leader of the Chorus of Old Women; but it is difficult to see how so important a person could disappear into the ignominy of captivity. I have preferred to envisage her as a straying member of the Chorus who has fallen into the hands of the Old Men.

35: *troops for Sicily:* A reference to the elaborate Sicilian Expedition (416 B.C.), in which Athens suffered a calamitous defeat from which she never recovered. (See note on DEMOSTRATOS.)

44: *"War's / a man's affair":* Quoted from *Iliad* VI:492; Hektor to Andromachê.

54: *I bore the holy vessels:* Annually, four girls of high birth, between the ages of seven and eleven, were appointed acolytes to Athenê in the Akropolis.

54: *I was pounding out the barley:* At the age of ten, an aristocratic girl was eligible to be chosen as Mill-maid; her duty was to grind the sacred grain for Athenê.

54: *Little Bear:* See note on BRAURON.

54: *Basket-Carrier:* The highest distinction of all. According to Σ, the baskets containing objects sacred to Athenê were of solid gold.

54: *Glory of the Persian Wars:* A sum of money, originally contributed by Athens and her allies, intended to finance an extension of the sea-war against Persia. Since the failure of the Sicilian Expedition, the contributions of the allies had fallen off; and the fund itself was now being raided by Athenian politicians.

55: *they fancy themselves as cavalry:* Sens. obsc.

59: *It isn't easy to say it, &c:* Σ says that this is 'from Euripides'; if so, it is from one of his lost plays.

60: *Pan's cave:* A grotto on the north side of the Akropolis, beneath the walls.

60: *the nearest brothel:* The proprietor was one Orsilochos.

62: *I dreamed / of a snake:* This divine Snake was the Guardian of the Temple, the peculiar Safeguard of the Akropolis. He never appeared; but each month a succulent cake was set out for him, and it always vanished overnight. The dreamer here has obviously been anticipating Freud.

63: *Those horrible owls:* The Owl was sacred to Athenê.

63: *The Oracle:* In translating this Oracle, I have aimed at a mystifying diction, a sing-song metre, and a foolish rime; that is to say, I have tried to sound like an Oracle. The meaning is studiously ambiguous; but the delighted interpolation of the First Woman makes it unnecessary, I hope, to analyse the entire Message.

77: *Oh, this mother business!:* A parody of Euripides, *Iph. Aul.* 917.

95: *Where a hotter fire?:* Parodied from the *Hippolytos* of Euripides.

95: *I'm through with women for ever!:* Also parodied from the *Hippolytos.*

96: *Can't live with them, or without them!:* Imitated by Martial in a famous epigram:

> *Difficilis, facilis, jucundus, acerbus es idem:*
> *nec tecum possum vivere, nec sine te.*

123

102: *looking for prominent statues:* The statues were the Hermai, stone posts set up in various parts of Athens. Just before the sailing of the Sicilian Expedition, a group of anonymous vandals mutilated these statues by chiseling off the heads and the protuberant *phalloi*. This and the women's Adonis-dirge (see note on ADONIS) were considered unhappy auguries.

103: *Summon Lysis-anybody!:* He actually says 'Lysistratos,' grasping at random for a name. Lysistrata's name means Dissolver of Armies.

104: *our husbands have been lax:* Apparently a reference to an earlier occasion when Sparta proposed terms to Athens, only to be rejected.

104: *this is* PEACE: Or, more accurately, Reconciliation. From here on, the stage business is largely a matter of guesswork, and this is one of the hazier guesses. Lysistrata has already asked 'Where is that goddess of Peace?' and it seems reasonable to suppose that someone should fetch her. But in what form? Some authorities prefer a disscreet Usherette who will assign the Athenians and the Lakonians to their proper stations about Lysistrata. Others prescribe a nude young woman. Still others (to whom for practical reasons I feel that I must adhere, much as I admire the downrightness of the second group) suggest such a statue as I have described in the stage direction. The nudity is all-important, for the abstracted replies of Athenians and Spartans alike depend upon their preoccupation with this image of Peace.

106: *Hog Island, &c:* These are all sexual equivocations, though the places themselves are real. Echinos (the word means Hedgehog) was near Thermopylai; 'the gulf' seems self-explanatory; and the Legs of Megara was a fortified corridor connecting Megara with its seaport, Nisaia. Unimportant places; their only significance here lies in their application to the person of Peace.

107: *and plow our fields:* See Sophokles, *Antigonê* 569. But the image is common.

117: *Athenê of the House of Brass:* This famous temple stood on the Akropolis of Sparta.

124

INDEX OF PROPER NAMES

ACHARNAI: A town in Attika.

ADONIS: A Phoenician fertility god whose cult became common in Greece. The *Adonia* was an annual two-day celebration of his death and resurrection, participated in exclusively by women, and generally on the flat house-tops. On the day of the departure of Nikias' fleet for the disastrous Sicilian Expedition, the women of Athens were wailing the Adonis-dirge ('Αδωνιασμός), and this was taken to be an evil omen.

AISCHYLOS: Greek tragic poet (*c.* 525-456 B.C.); the reference on p. 15 is to his *Seven Against Thebes*.

AKROPOLIS: The citadel of Athens, sacred to Athenê.

AMORGOS: An island in the Aegean a little southeast of Naxos; famed for the quality of its flax, of which the 'very thinnest gowns' mentioned by Lysistrata (p. 13) were made.

AMYKLAI: A town in Lakonia, the centre of the cult of Phoibos Apollo.

APHRODITE: Goddess of love.

APOLLO: The sun-god.

ARISTOGEITON: See HIPPIAS.

ARTEMESION: A promontory in Euboia; scene of a naval battle in which the Athenians successfully engaged the fleet of Xerxês.

ARTEMIS: Goddess of the chase; of virginity; of childbirth; of the moon; of wild animals; see BRAURON, PHOSPHOROS.

ATHENE: Goddess of wisdom; daughter of Zeus; tutelary goddess of Athens, where the Akropolis was sacred to her.

ATHENS: Chief city of the province of Attika, founded by Kekrops in 1550 B.C.

BOIOTIA: A country lying immediately north of Attika; noted for the crudity of its inhabitants (hence the reference on p. 9) and the excellence of its sea food, particularly its eels (p. 5).

BRAURON: A town on the eastern sea-coast of Attika where every five years the festival of Artemis Brauronia was celebrated. The symbol appropriate to it was the bear. According to Σ, some thoughtless young Athenians once killed a bear sacred to Artemis in her sanctuary at Brauron, and the oracle of the goddess proclaimed that the sacrilege could be atoned for only by having each young girl 'play the bear' once before the ages of five and ten respectively. The rite apparently involved walking in procession dressed in a saffron gown. But Iphigeneia was believed by some to have been sacrificed by her father Agamemnon at Brauron instead of at Aulis; and it will be remembered that she was dressed in saffron robes for the occasion. The subject seems desperately obscure.

CHARON: The 'gloom-bearded god' who sculled the souls of the newly dead across the Styx to Hades. The reference on p. 50 involves another of Aristophanes' many parodies of Euripides: in *Alkestis* the dying Queen cries

> *I see the dark lake,*
> *The boat in shore,*
> *And Charon holding the double oar, calling,*
> *'Why are you waiting, Alkestis? Come,*
> *'You are holding us back. . . .'*

DELPHOI: A town on the southwest side of Mt. Parnassos; also called Pytho; famous for its shrine of Pythian Apollo, one of the most powerful of Greek oracles. Here, every five years, were celebrated the Pythian Games, in honor of the god.

DEMETER: The earth-goddess.

DEMOSTRATOS: An Athenian orator and jingoist politician.

DIONYSOS: The god of wine.

DOG-FOX: The nickname of one Philostratos, eminent in this *métier*.

EILEITHYIA: Goddess of childbirth; *cf.* the Roman Juno Lucina.

EROS: God of love; son of Aphroditê.

EURIPIDES: Greek tragic poet (480-405 B.C.). In spite of such unusually 'feminist' plays as *Alkestis* and *Trojan Women,* he was renowned as a misogynist.

EUROTAS: A river of Sparta; see LEDA.

FURIES: The three goddesses of infernal vengeance.

GENETYLLIS: A name applied to Aphroditê as goddess of procreation (Σ); in the plural, more broadly, the minor deities attendant upon the goddess. Lysistrata (p. 3) refers to some kind of woman-festival, probably esoteric, in honor of this divinity.

GORGON: Here (p. 46) the reference is to Medusa, a woman-monster whose face had the power of turning to stone whoever looked upon it. Lysistrata's General has hopefully adorned his shield with a portrait of Medusa.

GRACES: Aglaia, Thalia, and Euphrosynê, daughters of Zeus and Herê; they symbolize all the candor and loveliness of women which men desire 'when pain and anguish wring the brow.'

HEKATE: Generally, a goddess of witchcraft; assimilated to several other deities, as Selenê in heaven, Artemis on earth, and Persephonê in Hadês: hence represented as *Triformis* (with three bodies) or *Triceps* (with three heads).

HELLAS: Greece.

HERE: Sister and wife of Zeus.

HERAKLES: The all-but-invincible Strong Man of Greek legend, son of Zeus and Alkmenê. Kinesias' outburst on p. 81 has a double intent: (1) as referring to a hardship, or 'Labor,' which even Heraklês would find intolerable; (2) as referring to many genial legends of Heraklês, the mighty eater, invited to dinner and then comically cheated of his food.

HIPPIAS: The last of the Tyrants of Athens. He reigned with his brother Hipparchos until the assassination of the former at the hands of the patriots Aristogeiton and Harmodios; driven into exile, he took refuge in Persia and was finally killed at Marathon (490 B.C.) fighting against his own country.

HOG ISLAND: See General Notes, under p. 106.

ISMENIA: The Boiotian aristocrat introduced to Lysistrata on p. 9.

KARYSTIANS: Inhabitants of Karystos, a town in southern Euboia. Though allies of Athens at this time, they were regarded with distaste for their primitive etiquette and uninhibited morals.

KASTOR: A son of Zeus and Leda; brother of Helen (of Troy) and Klytaimestra (wife of Agamemnon). He and his brother Polydeukês were the Heavenly Twins, tutelary spirits of Sparta.

KIMON: An Athenian general, sent with an expeditionary force to the aid of Sparta (see PERIKLEIDES).

KLEISTHENES: A decadent Athenian of ambisexual tendencies mentioned (p. 53) as the ideal plotter between the Athenian women and the Lakonian men; mentioned unmentionably (p. 102).

KLEOMENES: A king of Sparta who spent a great deal of his eccentric life intervening in Athenian politics. In 508 B.C., after a more or less abortive attempt to restore Isagoras to power, Kleomenês seized the Akropolis. With Isagoras, he was besieged there for two days by the Athenians; on the third, he and his men were allowed to depart for Sparta under a truce. (See Herodotos V: 69-73.) Since this event occurred ninety-seven years before the action of the *Lysistrata,* it is obvious that the Chorus could not have participated. Here, as elsewhere, Aristophanes employs his Chorus as a kind of civic memory incarnate (see LEIPSYDRION, MARATHON). The description (p. 24) of Kleomenês' disreputable exit is clearly a bit of patriotic wishful thinking: apparently the general marched out with the honors of war.

KLEPSYDRA: A sacred spring beneath the walls of the Akropolis, near

Pan's Cave; Kinesias' suggestion (p. 80) has overtones of blasphemy.

KORINTH: A city of Greece, situated on the isthmus connecting Attika with The Peloponnesos. Σ learnedly remarks that Korinth had more than its share of lewd women.

KORYBANTES: Priests of the Phrygian goddess Kybelê: emasculate, frenetic in behavior, given to the clashing of cymbals and the beating of drums.

KRANAOS: Second King of Athens, succeeding Kekrops.

KYPRIAN: A name for Aphroditê.

LAKONIA: A country in The Peloponnesos: chief city, Sparta.

LEDA: Wife of Tyndareus, King of Sparta. While bathing in the River Eurotas, she was approvingly observed by Zeus, who descended to her in the shape of a Swan. Of this union were born quadruplets: two daughters, Helen and Klytaimestra, and two sons, Kastor and Polydeukês.

LEIPSYDRION: After the assassination of Hipparchos, the Patriots were forced to flee from Athens. They fortified Leipsydrion, on the slopes of Mt. Parnês; but after a gallant and bloody defense, they were forced to surrender. Since this event took place about a century before the action of the *Lysistrata*, the participation of our Chorus is patently impossible. (See notes on KLEOMENES, MARATHON.)

LEMNOS: An island in the Aegean, opposite the Troad. Hephaistos crashed there in flames when he was hurled down from Olympos. 'Lemnos-fire' seems to be dragged in chiefly for the sake of a poor pun: Λήμνιον ← λῆμαι, Lemnian, and sore eyes. Σ, however, has two further suggestions: (1) the women of Lemnos were lewd; (2) Hephaistos established a smithy there.

LYKON'S WIFE: According to Σ, a certain Rhodia, who was much lampooned for her licentiousness. But the Greek text—τὴν Λύκωνος— is deliberately ambiguous, and could just as well mean Lysistrata.

MAENADS: Ecstatic women in the train of Dionysos, *q.v.*

MARATHON: A battle (490 B.C.) in which 10,000 Athenians, with 1,000

Plataian allies, defeated·a Persian force of enormously superior numbers. (For the surrealistic chronological implications of this passage, see the note on KLEOMENES.)

MEGARA: See General Notes, under p. 106.

MELANION: Nothing is known of this paragon beyond what the Old Men tell us in this strophê. There seems also to have been a proverb: 'as pure as Melanion.'

MESSENIA: A maritime country of The Peloponnesos, bounded on the north by Elis and Arkadia, and on the west by Lakonia. See PERIKLEIDES.

MIKON: The reference is to the prehistoric myth of an invasion of Attika by the Amazones (see General Notes, under p. 16) which was checked by Theseus under the walls of the Akropolis. Mikôn was one of several celebrated painters who dealt in the grand manner with this theme.

MILESIAN: An inhabitant of Miletos, a city of Caria, in northwestern Asia Minor. Miletos had abandoned the Athenian cause shortly before the *Lysistrata* was composed—hence Lysistrata's outburst on p. 10; but there is also an indelicate reference to a phallic apparatus reputedly manufactured there.

MNEMOSYNE: Goddess of Memory; mother, by Zeus, of the Muses: that is to say, the memory of the past engenders the arts and sciences of the present.

MYRONIDES: One of the most brilliant of the Athenian generals: *fl.* some forty years before the *Lysistrata*. The characteristic mentioned here (pp. 67-68) was supposed to be a sign of military excellence; hence the Old Women's deprecatory reference to it.

OLYMPIA: The Olympian Games.

PAN: A rural Arkadian god, associated with the worship of Bacchos in that province; a god of lascivious and mischievous tendencies (hence the reference on p. 90).

PANDRASOS: One of the daughters of Kekrops, the founder of Athens; used on p. 37 as a lady-like oath.

PAPHIAN: A name for Aphroditê.

PEISANDROS: A reckless and mercenary intriguer who, at the moment Aristophanes wrote, was bringing to success his plot to overthrow the Athenian democracy and establish in its place the hateful rule of the Four-Hundred.

PELOPONNESIAN: An inhabitant of The Peloponnesos, the southern part of Greece, at war with Athens from 431 to 404 B.C.

PERIKLEIDES: In 464 B.C., after an earthquake ('the sea-god splitting your shores') which devastated most of Sparta, the helots rebelled, and were supported in their insurgency by troops from Messenia. Sparta sent an ambassador, Perikleidês, to Athens, urging assistance. Athens obliged by sending Kimôn with 4,000 hoplites to the aid of the distressed city. (For the story, see Thucydidês I: 102.)

PHOIBOS: God of the sun.

PHOSPHOROS: Artemis in her 'aspect' as moon-goddess.

POSEIDON: God of the sea; on p. 35, an appropriate oath, when one considers the recent drenching.

PYLOS: A town in Messenia, on the west coast of The Peloponnesos.

RHODIAN: Pertaining to Rhodes, an island off the northwestern coast of Asia Minor. Perfume was manufactured here, but was apparently less esteemed than perfume from further east. There may be (p. 83) a derogatory political reference; but if so, it is too obscure for recovery.

SALAMIS: A large island in the Saronic Gulf, south of Attika.

SAMOS: An island in the Aegean, off the coast of Asia Minor. At the time of this play, the military liaison between Samos and Athens was very strong; the Samians supplied many excellent generals and ships to the Athenian cause.

SKYTHIANS: The Athenian police force was made up largely of Skythian archers. The Magistrate (p. 38) arrives at the Akropolis accompanied by four. On p. 15, Lysistrata's 'Inner Guard' is a whimsy of the poet's: 'Where's our Skythian-ess?'

SPARTA: The capital city of Lakonia; chief rival, and ultimate conqueror, of Athens.

STYX: The river of the dead; see CHARON.

TAURIAN: An epithet of the goddess Artemis, who was worshipped at Taurica Chersonesos: *i.e.,* the modern Crimea.

TAYGETOS: A mountain range in Lakonia, overhanging Sparta.

THASIAN: A fragrant and highly prized wine from the island of Thasos, in the northern Aegean.

THEAGENES: A citizen of Acharnai, so superstitious that he never left home without first consulting his household shrine of Hekatê. On p. 7 this peculiarity is transferred to his wife.

THERMOPYLAI: The 'Hot Gates': A narrow pass between Thessaly and Lokris, where in 480 B.C. an army of 300 Spartans under Leonidas held out for three days against an enormously superior Persian army.

THRACE: Broadly, all the country north of the Black Sea.

TIMON: A celebrated Athenian misanthrope. There is no reason, aside from the 'slanted' chatter of the Old Women, to believe that he excepted women from general hatred of mankind. (See Shakspere's *Timon of Athens.*)

ZEUS: Father of gods and men.

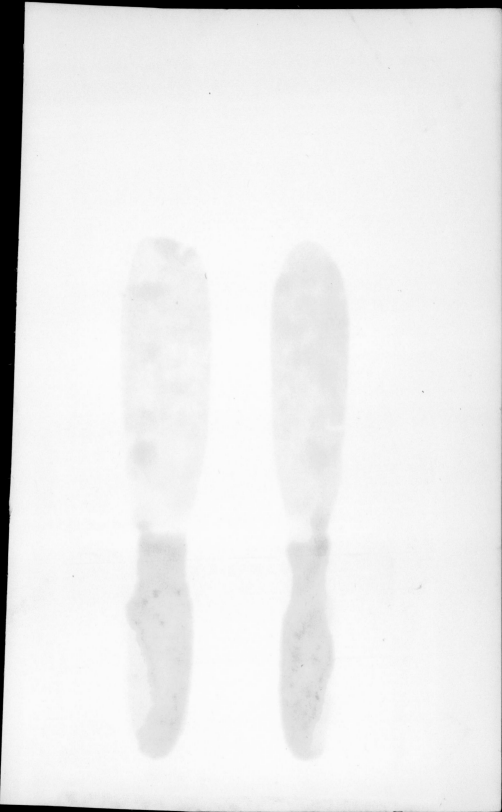

DATE DUE	
MAY 0 6 1998	
DEC 05 2003	
MAY 1 0 2005	
MAY 0 2 2006	
JUL 30 2012	
DEC 19 2018	

GAYLORD   PRINTED IN U.S.A.